DISCOVERING
ANCIENT
CHINA

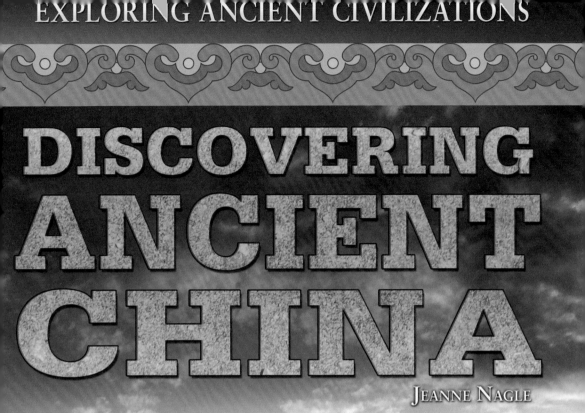

DISCOVERING ANCIENT CHINA

JEANNE NAGLE

Britannica
Educational Publishing

IN ASSOCIATION WITH

ROSEN
EDUCATIONAL SERVICES

Published in 2015 by Britannica Educational Publishing (a trademark of Encyclopædia Britannica, Inc.) in association with The Rosen Publishing Group, Inc.
29 East 21st Street, New York, NY 10010

Distributed exclusively by Rosen Publishing.
To see additional Britannica Educational Publishing titles, go to rosenpublishing.com.

First Edition

Britannica Educational Publishing
J. E. Luebering: Director, Core Reference Group
Anthony L. Green: Editor, Compton's by Britannica

Rosen Publishing
Hope Lourie Killcoyne: Executive Editor
Jacob R. Steinberg: Editor
Nelson Sá: Art Director
Nicole Russo: Designer
Cindy Reiman: Photography Manager
Karen Huang: Photo Researcher

Library of Congress Cataloging-in-Publication Data

Nagle, Jeanne.
Discovering ancient China/Jeanne Nagle.—First edition.
     pages cm.—(Exploring ancient civilizations)
Includes bibliographical references and index.
ISBN 978-1-62275-821-0 (library bound) — ISBN 978-1-62275-820-3 (pbk.) —
ISBN 978-1-62275-819-7 (6-pack)
1. China—History—To 1766 B.C.—Juvenile literature. 2. China—History—1766 B.C.-220 A.D.—Juvenile literature. 3. China—Civilization—Juvenile literature. I. Title.
DS741.5.N34 2015
931—dc23
                                                                                    2014027330

Manufactured in the United States of America.

Photo credits:
Cover, pp. 1, 3 feiyuezhangjie/Shutterstock.com; p. 7 Adapted from A. Herrmann, 'An Historical Atlas of China' (1966); Aldine Publishing Company; p. 9 TAO Images Limited/Getty Images; pp. 10, 41 Heritage Images/Hulton Archive/Getty Images; p. 12 Keren Su/China Span/Getty Images; p. 14 Musee Guimet,t, Paris, France/De Agostini Picture Library/Bridgeman Images; p. 16 Universal Images Group/Getty Images; pp. 19, 27, 37 Courtesy Minneapolis Institute of Arts; p. 20 from San-ts'ai-t'u-hui by Wang Ch'i; p. 23 Stuart Dee/Photographer's Choice/Getty Images; p. 24 DEA/G. Dagli Orti/De Agostini Picture Library/ Getty Images; p. 25 Hulton Archive/Getty Images; p. 29 O. Louis Mazzatenta/National Geographic Image Collection/Getty Images; p. 30 Luis Castaneda Inc./The Image Bank/Getty Images; p. 33 Sovfoto/ Universal Images Group/Getty Images; p. 34 lzf/Shutterstock.com; p. 36 British Library, London, UK/ Bridgeman Images; p. 39 © TopFoto/The Image Works; p. 40 © RMN-Grand Palais/Art Resource, NY; cover and interior graphics kornilov007/Shutterstock.com (patterned banners and borders), HorenkO/ Shutterstock.com and Freckles/Shutterstock.com (background textures).

CONTENTS

INTRODUCTION

Human ancestors lived in what is now China at least four hundred thousand years ago. Archaeologists have dug up tools and other objects in the Beijing area that were used by people in the Stone Age. Other proof of prehistoric civilizations has been found throughout China. The bones of human ancestors and early modern humans have been discovered, along with the remains of artifacts—the items they made. These pieces include tools carved from stone and animal bones. Evidence suggests that early people in China knew how to make and use fire.

Modern excavations give us a look into prehistoric China—a great civilization whose mysteries have been revealed through artifacts and other archaeological finds. In addition, most of the period known as ancient China (roughly 2000 BCE to 221 CE) is documented in written records. Artifacts reveal to us when the people of ancient China started to live in settled groups—at first mainly near the Huang He, or Yellow River. Eventually those settled groups formed communities. Dynasties (or royal families) began to rule over these communities.

The story of ancient China is defined by the history, emperors, culture, and traditions of its various dynasties. By relating the details behind China's early dynastic empires, this book opens a portal to one of antiquity's most important civilizations.

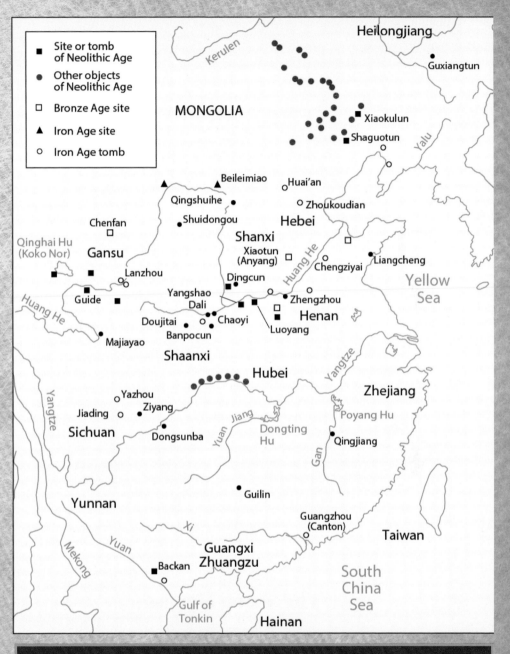

■	Site or tomb of Neolithic Age
●	Other objects of Neolithic Age
□	Bronze Age site
▲	Iron Age site
○	Iron Age tomb

Heilongjiang

Kerulen

Guxiangtun

MONGOLIA

Xiaokulun

Shaguotun

Yalu

Beileimiao

Huai'an

Qingshuihe

Zhoukoudian

Chenfan

Shuidongou

Hebei

Qinghai Hu (Koko Nor)

Gansu

Shanxi

Xiaotun (Anyang)

Liangcheng

Chengziyai

Huang He

Lanzhou

Dingcun

Yellow Sea

Guide

Yangshao

Dali

Zhengzhou

Huang He

Doujitai

Chaoyi

Henan

Banpocun

Luoyang

Majiayao

Shaanxi

Hubei

Yazhou

Ziyang

Zhejiang

Jiading

Poyang Hu

Sichuan

Dongsunba

Yuan Jiang

Dongting Hu

Qingjiang

Yangtze

Gan

Guilin

Yunnan

Xi

Guangzhou (Canton)

Taiwan

Yuan

Guangxi Zhuangzu

Mekong

Backan

South China Sea

Gulf of Tonkin

Hainan

The principal settlements of ancient China were located along the country's major rivers, the Yangtze and the Huang He.

CHAPTER ONE

THE EARLY DYNASTIES

The first dynasty in ancient China was the Xia. However, the Xia kings, who reportedly ruled from about 2070 to 1600 BCE, are mentioned only in legends. They may not have actually existed. According to legend, the founder of the Xia dynasty was Yu the Great. Yu was credited with draining the waters of a great flood and introducing irrigation to ancient China. His contributions made him a lord of the harvest. Tradition gives the names of the dynasty's successive rulers, ending with Jie. Jie is said to have fallen in love with a beautiful but evil woman who acted cruelly. The story says that the outraged people rose up in rebellion. Tradition tells that the leader of this rebellion, Zi Lü, became the first ruler of the next great dynasty: the Shang.

The Shang Dynasty

Until the 1920s, many experts believed that the Shang dynasty might also be a legend, like the Xia. However,

This sculpture in Chongqing, China, shows Yu the Great (*center*) ridding the land of floodwaters.

archaeologists discovered many artifacts that helped prove the dynasty's existence. These artifacts include bones and shells carved with Chinese characters. Thanks to these interesting finds, the Shang dynasty is the first recorded Chinese dynasty for which there is both written and archaeological evidence. The Shang created one of the

Ancient Chinese characters cover the base of a tortoise shell believed to date back to the Shang dynasty.

earliest advanced civilizations in East Asia. Culturally the dynasty is most noted for its bronze tools and written documents.

ARCHAEOLOGY AND ANCIENT WORLDS

Apart from written records and carved inscriptions, knowledge about ancient peoples is derived from the work of archaeologists. Most of the significant archaeological findings have been made in the past two hundred years. Some of the most important archaeological digs in China were made after the late 1970s.

Weapons, pottery, and muscial instruments are some of the more common archaeological finds, but other surprising discoveries have been made. In 2002 a set of four-thousand-year-old noodles were unearthed at Lajia, an archaeological site in the Qinghai Province of northwestern China. The noodles—made from a type of grain called millet—were the oldest noodles ever discovered!

Location and Type of Rule

Historians think that the Shang kings ruled from about 1600 to 1046 BCE. The Shang state did not cover the entire territory that now makes up China. It was centered in the North China Plain and extended as far north as modern Shandong and Hebei Provinces and westward through present Henan Province.

During the time of the Shang, the land was governed by a number of tribes or clans that were overseen by a king from one of the dominant, or most powerful, clans. The king was believed to have direct

Chariots and animal bones, uncovered in the ruins of the Shang capital of Anyang, are on display in the Yinxu Museum (Henan Province).

contact with the spirit world, from which he received his power. Historians estimate that approximately thirty kings ruled during the Shang dynasty.

The kings of the Shang are believed to have occupied several capitals one after another. One possible site is modern Zhengzhou, in Henan Province, where there are rich archaeological finds. The Shang eventually settled at Anyang, also, in what is now Henan Province, in the 1300s BCE.

Shang Contributions

The Shang made a number of important and lasting contributions to Chinese society. They created a highly developed calendar system with a 360-day year with twelve months of thirty days each. It was during the Shang period that Chinese writing began to develop. No works of literature survive from the Shang dynasty, but numerous records and ceremonial writing as well as family or clan names exist. Many were carved into or brushed onto bones or tortoise shells. Three kinds of characters were used, and they represent the earliest known forms of writing in China.

ORACLE BONES

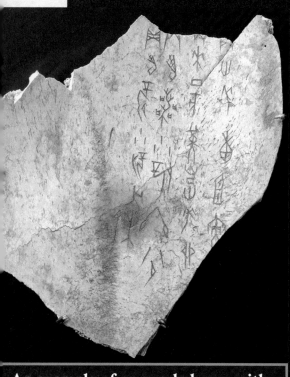

An example of an oracle bone, with characters that were believed to ward off danger scratched into the shoulder bone of an ox.

Ox bones and tortoise shells with ancient writing on them have been unearthed in parts of China. They are referred to as oracle bones. Archaeologists believe they were used for fortune-telling and record keeping in ancient China. Apparently, characters were first brushed on a bone in red or black ink. They were then traced over with a sharp instrument. Heat was applied, causing the bone to crack. People of the time believed that the crack patterns could be read as a way of telling what would happen in the future.

Bronze, Pottery, and Jade

The Shang excelled in bronze work. While the earliest bronzes of the Shang were primitive, they eventually grew more advanced.

Later Shang bronze works included elegant ceremonial objects. Notable was a substantial range of cooking and serving dishes, as well as various utensils and ornaments. Some bronze weapons have been found, too.

Pottery objects were abundant. Some of the pottery seems to have even been shaped on a potter's wheel. Pottery included dishes and bowls in a white glaze for ceremonial and ritual use and black pottery in a rich brown glaze for more everyday purposes.

In addition, jade carving became quite advanced during the Shang dynasty. Ceremonial weapons of jade were made, as well as jade fittings for actual weapons. Jade figurines included both human and animal shapes carved in the round in careful detail. Many of these jade objects were found in tombs of the period.

Keeping and Losing Power

Using bronze weapons gave the Shang army an advantage in warfare. Invaders from outside the Shang state—and even several clans within the state who wanted to take power away from the ruling clan—had inferior weapons made of weaker materials. The Shang fought both to keep invaders out

This bronze cooking pot dates back to the Shang dynasty.
Notice the special carvings on the pot and its lid.

of their territory and to gain more land and treasures for themselves.

When a Shang king called Dixin (also known as Zi Zhou) became extremely corrupt, the dynasty fell apart. Dixin was a cruel ruler who covered trees of the forest with the flesh of his enemies or anyone who dared to oppose him. The people resented paying taxes so that the king could build the elaborate Deer Tower Palace, which had doors and entire chambers constructed of precious stones.

According to traditional Chinese history, the way Dixin ruled caused him to lose the favor of heaven, which made him vulnerable and weak. Because of this, the Shang met their downfall in the 1000s BCE from the nearby Zhou kingdom.

CHAPTER TWO
THE REIGN OF THE ZHOU

Sometime around 1050 BCE, the Zhou kingdom led the armies of several other states into a great battle against the Shang—and won. The Zhou dynasty remained in power for almost eight hundred years.

Historians divide the long rule of the Zhou dynasty into two separate periods: Early and Late. The two periods are more formally named after the location of the dynasty's capital. From 1046 to 771 BCE, which is the Early Zhou period, the capital was near the modern city of Xi'an. In 771, after an invasion by people to the north, the capital was moved farther east, to what is now the city of Luoyang. The two periods are thus also known as the Western Zhou and the Eastern Zhou.

The Western Zhou

The Western Zhou Dynasty ruled over most of the North China Plain, as well as land south into the Yangtze River valley. Some two hundred states came

CHINA
Zhou Dynasty
1046 - 256 BCE

Land under rule

Current political
boundaries

Kilometers
0 ———————— 500
0 ———————— 500
Miles

The map above indicates the extent of the Zhou dynasty compared
to the modern borders of China.

under the rule of a central government, headed by the king. Overseeing each state were local nobles who were loyal to the king. In fact, many of these nobles were part of the king's extended family.

Power came from the top down in a political and social system that was similar to the feudal system that occurred much later in Europe. The upper classes, or aristocracy, were lords who ruled in each state. Under them were ministers and officers who helped run the state governments and maintain peace. Military "knights" were among the people who came next. At the bottom of the social system were the everyday citizens, mostly peasant farmers who worked the land on behalf of the ruling lord.

This ink drawing depicts the Duke of Zhou.

The Duke of Zhou

One of the most admired rulers in Chinese history lived during the Western Zhou dynasty. His name was Zhougong, which means "the Duke of Zhou."

The duke helped his brother Wuwang gather enough power to defeat the Shang and to found the Zhou dynasty. Instead of grabbing power for himself when his brother died, the duke became regent, or temporary ruler, and advisor for Wuwang's young son. This move angered two of Zhougong's surviving brothers, who thought he was trying to steal the throne for himself. The brothers hatched a plot with rebels from the defeated Shang dynasty to overthrow Zhougong, but the duke quickly put a stop to the rebellion.

During his time as regent, the Duke of Zhou helped bring the many states closer together. He did this by creating political and social systems that everyone in the country was required to follow. The administrative framework he helped establish served as a model for future Chinese dynasties.

At the end of seven years, when the young king finally came of age, Zhougong stepped down as regent—just as he said he would—and gave power to Wuwang's son. This act shows why the Duke of Zhou is greatly respected. He was a man of honor who lived up to his promises.

THE FIVE CLASSICS

The Duke of Zhou was said to be a good poet. It is fitting, then, that one of the first classics of Chinese literature, the *Shijing* (Classic of Poetry), was published during the rule of the dynasty he was instrumental in building. The book is a collection of

(*continued on the next page*)

(*continued from the previous page*)

305 poems that were originally sung to the accompaniment of music. Among them are folk ballads, courtly songs, and songs of praise. Most were already hundreds of years old at the time they were compiled, in about the 6th century BCE.

The *Shijing* is one of the *Wujing* (Five Classics) of Chinese literature. The others are the *Liji* (Collection of Rituals), a book of rituals; the *Shujing* (Classic of History), a collection of historical documents; the *Chunqiu* (Spring and Autumn [Annals]), a history of the state where the philosopher Confucius was born; and the *Yijing* (Classic of Changes), a famous philosophical guide. All the books of the *Wujing* are associated in some way with Confucius, who is thought to have compiled or edited some of them.

Advances in Farming and Water Control

The economy of the Zhou state was centered mainly on farming. Because it was their chief occupation, the Zhou found ways to make growing and harvesting food easier and more efficient. The farmers practiced crop rotation, in which fields are planted with a certain crop in one season and a different one in another season. New crops, including soybeans, were also introduced during this period.

The Three Gorges Dam, the world's largest hydroelectric dam, was built along China's Yangtze River. The use of dams and reservoirs in China dates back to the Zhou dynasty, when they were used to control flooding along the river, not to provide power.

Irrigation systems were put into place, to make farms more productive. The Huang He and the Yangtze River were prone to overflowing their banks, causing a lot of damage to communities in the river valleys. Therefore, the Zhou made flood control a priority. During this period water tanks and reservoirs (which held water for public use) were also built, and canals were dug.

A Time of War

The Eastern, or Late, Zhou dynasty is divided into two separate periods. The first, known as the Spring and Autumn period (770–476 BCE),

This display shows bronze swords and arrowheads dating back to ancient China's Warring States period.

saw iron replace bronze as the metal of choice for making tools and weapons. During this time, there was an increase in agricultural production and also a rise in the number of battles fought between neighboring states within China.

Increasing conflict led to what is known as the Warring States period, which began in 475 BCE. Although the Zhou dynasty ended in 256 BCE, the Warring States period continued until 221 BCE. Years of fighting led to many changes during this period, including in how and why wars in China were fought. Also, scholars became very important at this time. They worked mainly as tutors, teaching the children of the most powerful families, and also as advisors to government officials. The philosopher Confucius was one of these scholars.

Confucius

Confucius is regarded as one of the most important people in ancient Chinese civilization. He was born in 551 BCE in Qufu, in what is now China's Shandong Province. His family name was Kong. Confucius is a European version of the Chinese name Kongfuzi, meaning "Master Kong."

Confucius began teaching while in his thirties. His goal was to improve society. He believed that students should work on bettering their characters in addition to gaining knowledge. Confucius was also concerned with politics. He held government posts in his forties and fifties but never received a position of great influence. Confucius died in 479 BCE. His teachings, which emphasized kindness, love, respect, loyalty, and obedience, were deeply influential throughout eastern Asia.

A central figure in ancient Chinese history, Confucius put forth highly influential ideas about how people should live. His teachings, called Confucianism, have guided the Chinese people for more than two thousand years.

CONFUCIANISM AND DAOISM

Begun during the Zhou dynasty, both Confucianism and Daoism have helped to shape Chinese culture, serving as guidelines to proper human behavior. The teachings of Confucius, known collectively as Confucianism, hold that people are duty bound to each other on several levels. If each person's duties are continually met, then societies operate smoothly.

In contrast, the system of philosophy known as Daoism emphasizes being in harmony with nature. It teaches that all things are connected as one. It is considered to be more joyful and carefree than Confucianism. Both systems emphasize the importance of harmonious interaction.

A New Power Rises

During the Warring States period, seven individual states gained so much power from fighting that they began to challenge the king as ruler over all of China. The rebellion of these seven states caused the decline and fall of the Zhou dynasty. After the Zhou lost control, the most powerful state, the Qin, defeated the other six states and began a dynasty of its own.

CHAPTER THREE
THE QIN DYNASTY

From 770 to 221 BCE, during the rule of the Eastern Zhou dynasty, ancient China was divided into many small states. One of these states, the Qin, occupied the Wei River valley in the extreme northwestern area of the country. Beginning in the third century BCE, the Qin created a highly organized and powerful state. They gradually began to conquer their neighbors.

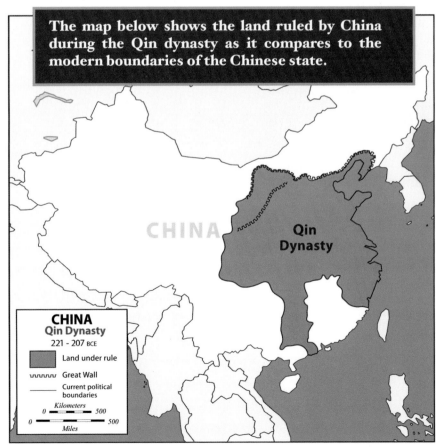

The map below shows the land ruled by China during the Qin dynasty as it compares to the modern boundaries of the Chinese state.

CHINA

Qin Dynasty

CHINA
Qin Dynasty
221 - 207 BCE

▨ Land under rule

ʌʌʌʌʌ Great Wall

—— Current political boundaries

Kilometers
0 ▬▬ 500

0 ▬▬ 500
Miles

The Qin dynasty was the first to unify China and establish the Chinese empire. The reign of the Qin was relatively short (221–207 BCE). Furthermore, their harsh methods of rule made them unpopular with their subjects. Nonetheless, the Qin created a lasting legacy: they established the basic boundaries and governing system that all subsequent Chinese dynasties were to follow for the next two thousand years.

NAMING RIGHTS

In addition to establishing many rules of governing, the Qin also left another notable legacy. It is widely believed that the word "China" itself comes from the name of the dynasty. (*Qin* is pronounced "chin.") Some scholars believe that variations of this dynasty's name made their way into Greek and Latin, eventually giving rise to the modern name by which China is identified in many languages.

Coming to Power

During the reign of the Zhou, the state of Qin had become increasingly wealthy and powerful. The state had leaders who formed a strong, central government with an army that defeated other states and took their land. The boy king Ying Zheng came to the Qin throne in 246 BCE. He ultimately completed the Qin conquests by defeating all the other states.

With his opponents beaten and powerless, Ying Zheng created the Qin empire in 221 BCE. He proclaimed himself Shihuangdi (First Sovereign Emperor). The term *emperor* was used for the first time in Chinese history to set Ying Zheng apart from the kings who had ruled when the country was split into smaller states. There were other ways in which the emperor showed his special position. He built huge, expensive palaces in which to live. Elaborate royal ceremonies further inspired awe in the people.

A statue of Shihuangdi—emperor during the Qin dynasty—stands in China's Shaanxi Province.

Government

The Qin presided over an empire that reached the Korean peninsula in the east, the Sichuan basin in the west, the Gobi Desert in the north, and the South China Sea in the south. To rule this vast territory, the Qin created a highly efficient system of government. They divided the empire into about forty provinces. Each province was ruled by a governor who reported to the

The Great Wall of China began as a forced public-works project designed to protect the Qin dynasty's many provinces.

king. They also built an elaborate highway network to link the provinces with the capital, Xianyang.

The Qin attempted to control nearly every aspect of life in the empire. Qin rulers standardized the writing system. They also standardized the measurements of length and weight and even the width of highways. While the Qin governed efficiently, they also ruled with a brutal hand. They kept order throughout their empire with the help of a large and well-trained army. The government also made the families who had previously ruled over Qin land move to the capital city—to keep track of them and to keep them in line. In addition, the Qin forced many citizens to perform manual labor for the state. They were made to work on projects ranging from roads and palaces to connecting sections of defensive walls. These connected wall segments eventually formed the Great Wall of China.

THE GREAT WALL OF CHINA

The Great Wall of China winds across the Chinese countryside for some 5,500 miles (8,850 kilometers). It is one of the biggest structures ever made by humans. Made of dirt, stone, and brick, it ranges from

(continued on the next page)

(continued from the previous page)

15 to 30 feet (5 to 9 meters) high and from 15 to 25 feet (5 to 8 meters) wide.

The ancient Chinese built the wall to protect against invading armies. Workers began constructing the Great Wall in the 600s BCE. It was built in several separate sections. In the 200s BCE, citizens of the Qin dynasty joined the sections together to make one long wall. Since that time the wall has been extended and rebuilt many times. Most of the wall that exists today was built in the 15th and 16th centuries, during the Ming dynasty.

The wall has openings at positions that were important in ancient times, such as places where the wall crossed trade routes. Each opening had a gate with a watchtower on top. Many watchtowers rise above the wall, and a roadway runs along the top.

The Chinese stopped using the wall for protection in the mid-1600s CE. Parts of it were rebuilt in the 1900s. Today the wall is a tourist attraction and a symbol of China.

The Fall of the Qin

Shihuangdi was an effective ruler, as far as creating a unified empire went. However, some of his actions made him unpopular. The Qin wanted to control everything, including knowledge. The emperor often found himself at odds with the Confucian scholars, who did

This painting shows the murder of Confucian scholars at the command of the Qin emperor Shihuangdi (*top, center*), who considered them a threat to his total power.

not approve of the way he ruled. In 213 BCE, he ordered the burning of all books that he thought threatened his power. The only books that were saved were those on

Shown here is just a portion of the terra-cotta army sculpted to guard the remains of Shihuangdi.

what he thought were useful subjects such as law, agriculture, and medicine. Further, he had scholars who opposed him killed or sent into exile.

Because he was disliked so intensely—he had survived at least three attempted murders—Shihuangdi felt threatened. To protect himself, he went into seclusion, meaning he withdrew from contact with the outside world. He spent time and money trying to find a way to live forever. Needless to say, he never found the secret to immortality. When Shihuangdi died in 210 BCE, he was buried in

A TERRA-COTTA GUARD

Shihuangdi's burial spot, known as the Qin tomb, is famous for its clay army. Accidentally discovered in 1974 by farmers drilling a well, the underground army includes some eight thousand life-size statues of warriors, including archers and foot soldiers. They are accompanied by four hundred figures of horses and one hundred chariots. The figures are very detailed and realistic, and they were fully painted before being placed in the tomb.

The clay soldiers were grouped into a specific military formation. This configuration had bowmen and crossbowmen in the front, outer files of archers, groups of infantrymen and charioteers, and an armored guard in the rear. This formation followed the military prescriptions of the time. The army also faced east, the direction of Shihuangdi's chief enemies.

a massive tomb that was guarded from inside by a life-size army of clay figures.

After Shihuangdi's death, rebellion erupted throughout the empire. In 207, rebels overthrew the new Qin leader. The following year they established the Han dynasty, which ruled China for roughly the next four hundred years.

CHAPTER FOUR
LIFE UNDER THE HAN

This drawing depicts the first Han emperor, Liu Bang.

In 221 BCE, the Qin had united vast China into one empire for the first time. But the Qin were harsh rulers. Rebels replaced the Qin with the new Han dynasty in 206 BCE. A few years later, a man named Liu Bang, one of the leaders of the rebellion, became the first Han emperor.

Han rulers made many changes and improvements to the government structure that had been set up by the Qin. Most important, they adopted Confucianism—a system of beliefs or way of life that places great importance on honesty and the humane treatment of others.

A Tale of Two Hans

Historians divide the Han dynasty into two periods: the Earlier (or Western) Han period began in 206 BCE and lasted until 9 CE, when a rebel named Wang Mang took power. In 25 CE, the Han dynasty was restored. The period from 25 to 220 CE is called the Later (or Eastern) Han. The Earlier Han was a time when China waged costly campaigns to defend against invasions in the north by

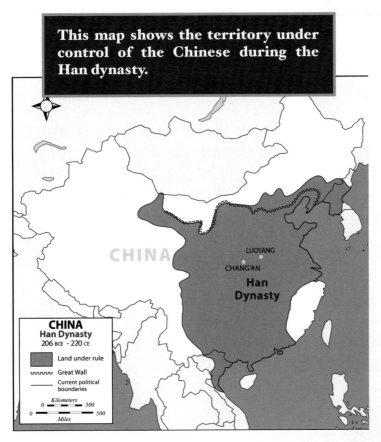

This map shows the territory under control of the Chinese during the Han dynasty.

CHINA
Han Dynasty
206 BCE - 220 CE

Land under rule

Great Wall

Current political boundaries

Kilometers
0 — 500
0 — 500
Miles

the Xiongnu, a fierce people of Central Asia. During the Later Han, warriors regained lost territories.

The alternate names for each period—Western and Eastern—refer to a change in the site of the capital. During the first part of Han rule the capital was located in the western part of the empire, in the city of Chang'an (now Xi'an). The later Han capital was located in the city of Luoyang, to the east of Chang'an.

THE DYNASTY IN BETWEEN

In between the Western and Eastern Han dynasties was the short-lived Xin dynasty. The Xin was formed by Wang Mang, the nephew to a Western Han empress. He maneuvered his way into becoming regent to an infant emperor and then emperor himself in 9 CE.

During his short time as emperor, Wang Mang put forth a number of reforms that angered many citizens. He attempted to redistribute land more evenly among citizens, and his money reforms caused property values to decline. He also tried to implement an ineffective reform of tax policies. He was killed by rebels who stormed his palace in 23 CE. In Chinese history, he is known as Shehuangdi, the "Usurper Emperor."

Government

In many ways, the Han borrowed existing government systems that they essentially inherited from the Qin. They kept the various administrative areas of the country, which were ruled by the central government, intact. To that system, they added the concept of a civil service—a body of government officials who served in nonpolitical posts. The officials were civilians who were selected and promoted on the basis of ability, rather than politics. These qualified officials helped the government run smoothly. An imperial university was established to train and test civilians for these desired job posts.

This page is from *Lunyu*, an important written collection of Confucian ethical beliefs.

The Han also turned from Legalism to Confucianism as the country's official doctrine. Legalism was a Chinese philosophy that taught that human beings are inherently selfish and shortsighted. It relied on fear to control citizens. Legalism purported that if citizens were afraid of being severely punished, they would not go against the government. By contrast, Confucianism emphasizes personal virtue, or right behavior. The Han believed that by emphasizing personal virtue, citizens would obey the law and remain loyal to the government and to the emperor.

Han Culture

Promoting China's culture was extremely important to the Han leaders. The performing arts flourished. A government bureau, or department, compiled descriptions of the

马王堆三号汉墓出土导引图复原图

Experts believe that this drawing of figures, which dates back to the Han dynasty, is an exercise chart. It was found in a tomb in the 1970s.

music of the day. These descriptions listed the instruments and songs that were played as well as the techniques that were used. Dance was part of public ceremony and private entertainment. In drama, performers acted out the heroic deeds of China's great warriors.

The visual arts—that is, painting, sculpture, and design—also benefited under the Han regime. The interior walls of important buildings were painted with historical portraits and scenes. Sculptors used stone and

Created by a Chinese craftsman during the Western Han dynasty, this bronze basin features painted artwork.

41

bronze to carve lifelike figures of people and animals. Artisans of the Han era refined the lacquerware for which ancient China became known. Many layers of lacquer, or varnish, were applied to decorative and everyday objects made of clay and wood. This gave them a high gloss. Some lacquerware was inlaid with jade or ivory.

During the Han period, China made advancements in science and technology

ACHIEVEMENTS IN LITERATURE

The Han rulers actively promoted literature. The Five Classics—books that have long been used as guides for personal behavior, good government, and religious conduct—were restored to favor. Also, a music bureau was formed to collect folk songs, and traditional poetry flourished.

The literary masterpiece of the Han period was the *Shiji* (Historical Records), by Sima Qian. Sima Qian was an astronomer, a calendar expert, and the first great Chinese historian. His *Shiji* consisted of more than 520,000 words divided into 130 chapters. Covering a period of about two thousand years, it was the most thorough record of Chinese history ever completed at the time. The records took eighteen years to produce and were completed in about 85 BCE. A two-volume English translation, *Records of the Grand Historian of China*, was published in 1961.

(though the Western world did not learn of these innovations for some time). Chinese inventions of the period included paper, water clocks, sundials, locks for controlling water levels in streams, a seismograph for measuring the strength of earthquakes, and compasses. The Han people divided the day into ten and later twelve parts. They also worked out a calendar of moon cycles; it remained in use until 1912.

Conclusion

In 220 CE, internal power struggles brought an end to the Han dynasty, as well as to the country's unity. For the next forty-five years, the empire was divided into three kingdoms— the Wei, Shu-Han, and Wu. By 280 CE, a new dynasty called the Jin again reunited China, but the dynasty soon fell apart, and the country disintegrated into chaos. Despite the weak political structures, the Chinese made many advances in science, literature, and the arts during that time. After more than three and a half centuries of political disunity, China would be again reunited under the Sui dynasty. But with the end of the Han dynasty, the period commonly referred to as ancient China had indeed come to an end.

ARCHAEOLOGY A science that deals with past human life and activities by studying the bones, tools, and other remains of ancient people.

BUREAU A subdivision of a government department.

DYNASTY A family of rulers who rule over a country for a long period of time.

EMPEROR The leader of an empire, meaning a group of countries or regions.

FEUDAL Relating to or having the characteristics of feudalism, a system of political organization in Europe during the Middle Ages in which knights served lords and received protection and land in return.

IRRIGATION The watering of land by a man-made system to help plants grow.

LACQUER A material-like varnish that dries quickly into a shiny layer.

LEGALISM A school of Chinese philosophy emphasizing that citizens must strictly follow the law or suffer specific punishments.

LEGEND A story coming down from the past whose truth is popularly accepted but cannot be checked.

MINISTER A high official who heads a department of the government.

ORACLE A person or object that gives wise advice.

PORTAL A large or magnificent point of entry.

PRIMITIVE Of or having to do with the earliest age or period.

REFORMS Changes made in order to improve governments or societies.

REGENT Someone who governs a kingdom when the true ruler is not able to.

SCHOLAR Someone who studies under a teacher, or a person who has done advanced study in a special area.

TERRA-COTTA A glazed or unglazed baked clay that has a brownish-orange color.

VULNERABLE Open to attack or damage.

Bramwell, Neil D. *Discover Ancient China*. Berkeley Heights, NJ: Enslow Publishers, Inc., 2014.

Capek, Michael. *Secrets of the Terracotta Army: Tomb of an Ancient Chinese Emperor*. North Mankato, MN: Capstone Press, 2014.

Friedman, Mel. *Ancient China* (True Books: Ancient Civilizations). New York, NY: Scholastic, 2010.

Mah, Adeline Yen. *China: Land of Dragons and Emperors*. New York, NY: Random House, 2008.

Shaughnessy, Edward L. *Exploring the Life, Myth, and Art of Ancient China*. New York, NY: Rosen Publishing, 2009.

Steele, Philip. *Hands-On History: Ancient China*. Helotes, TX: Armadillo Children's Publishing, 2013.

Ting, Renee. *Chinese History Stories, Vol. 1: Stories from the Zhou Dynasty*. New York, NY: Shen's Books, 2009

Tsaing, Sarah. *Warriors and Wailers: One Hundred Ancient Chinese Jobs You Might Have Relished or Reviled*. Toronto, ON, Canada: Annick Press, 2012.

Websites

Because of the changing nature of Internet links, Rosen Publishing has developed an online list of websites related to the subject of this book. This site is updated regularly. Please use this link to access the list:

http://www.rosenlinks.com/ANCIV/China